D0606995

My Life as an Early Settler

Nancy Kelly Allen

rourkeeducationalmedia.com

Teacher Notes available at
rem4teachers.com

www.rourkeeducationalmedia.com

PHOTO CREDITS: Images courtesy of Plimoth Plantation, www.plimoth.org

Special thanks to Karin Goldstein, curator of Collections and Library at Plimoth Plantation for content consultation and images.

Edited by: Precious McKenzie
Cover design by: Tara Raymo
Interior design by: Renee Brady

Library of Congress EPCN Data

My Life as an Early Settler/Nancy Kelly Allen
(Little World Social Studies)
ISBN 978-1-61810-140-2(hard cover)(alk. paper)
ISBN 978-1-61810-273-7(soft cover)
Library of Congress Control Number: 2011945867

Rourke Educational Media
Printed in the United States of America,
North Mankato, Minnesota

rourkeeducationalmedia.com

customerservice@rourkeeducationalmedia.com • PO Box 643328 Vero Beach, Florida 32964

My family and I are **early settlers**. We are some of the first European people to sail to **America** to start a new life.

Early settlers came to America for many reasons. **Pilgrims** and Puritans came so they could practice their own religion.

Early European settlers built the colony of Jamestown, Virginia, in 1607.

Some early European settlers came to America to own land, or to hunt for gold, or to trap fur.

Early settlers came from many different countries and built their homes in the new land.

I came to **New England** in 1620 on the ship Mayflower. Some people called our group the Pilgrims.

The Pilgrams sailed from Plymouth, England, on a voyage across the Atlantic Ocean.

102 Pilgrims sailed for 66 days on a wooden ship.

We named our **settlement** Plymouth Plantation.

We agreed to work together.

Life was difficult. The winter was cold and snowy. We didn't have much to eat.

About half the Pilgrims died the first winter.

The Wampanoag tribe helped us in many ways. Since we did not know how to hunt and fish in the new land, they taught us.

The next spring life was better. We built houses. Each house often had only one room for the whole family.

The Pilgrims used fire to cook food and for heat in the cold winter.

A **Native American** named Squanto taught us how to grow corn and other plants to eat because the seeds we brought did not grow well.

We planted a dead fish with each corn seed to make the soil rich.

My mother taught me until I was six years old. When I grew older, my father taught me to read and write because we didn't have schools.

Ninepins

When we had leisure time, we played marbles, rolling hoops, whip the top, and ninepins.

Our first year was hard, but our corn grew and there were many animals to hunt. Thanks to Providence, we survived.

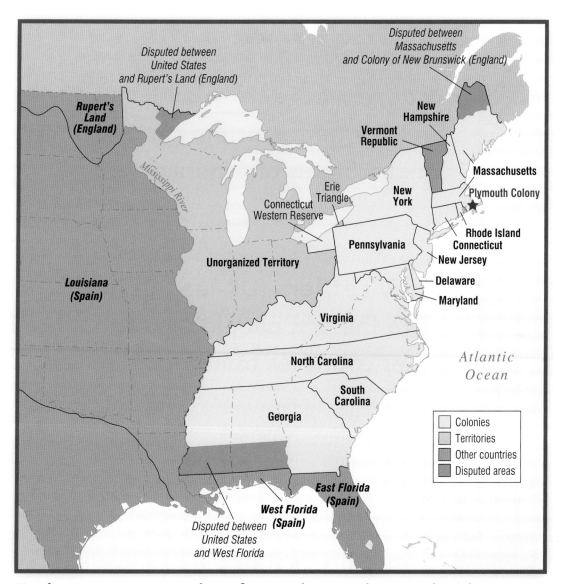

Early European settlers formed 13 colonies that became the United States of America.

Picture Glossary

 **America** (uh-MER-i-kuh): America is another name for the country of the United States of America.

 **early settlers** (UR-lee SET-lerz): They were the first people who came from other countries to America to live.

 **Native American** (NAY-tuv uh-MER-I-kan): Native Americans were the first people to live in America.

New England (NOOH ING-luhnd): The region in America where the Pilgrims settled.

Pilgrims (PIL-gruhms): The English settlers who came to America for religious freedom.

settlement (SET-l-muhnt): A small village with people and homes.

Index

Websites

www.fedstats.gov/kids/mapstats

www.plimoth.org//what-see-do/17th-century-english-village

www.smithsonianeducation.org/students/

About the Author

Nancy Kelly Allen enjoys reading and writing about the history of America. She also enjoys wearing an apron and bonnet when she attends events such as Old Fashion Days and Heritage Festivals. The clothes are fun to wear and remind her of the early settlers who wore aprons and bonnets daily.

Ask The Author!
www.rem4students.com